PROXIMITY

BEGINNER'S GUIDE TO TARGETED DIGITAL MARKETING

Introduction to Targeted Digital Marketing

In today's dynamic digital landscape, businesses of all sizes have unprecedented potential to reach their target consumers with precision and efficiency via targeted digital marketing. This strategic strategy entails adjusting marketing efforts to target specific parts of the population that are most likely to be interested in their products or services. This is in stark contrast to traditional mass marketing, which frequently entails broadcasting generalist messages to broad groups without the exact targeting requirements required for tailored digital efforts.

The proliferation of digital platforms and powerful analytics tools has transformed how organizations discover, understand, and communicate with their customers.

Businesses that use data analytics can acquire significant insights into consumer behaviors, tastes, and purchasing patterns. This allows marketers to divide their audience based on demographics (age, gender, geography, and income) as well as psychographics. Such segmentation enables the development of highly targeted marketing efforts adapted to the specific demands and goals of various customer categories.

Targeted digital marketing not only improves the relevance and efficacy of marketing campaigns, but it also optimizes resource allocation and maximizes return on investment (ROI). Businesses can reduce waste and increase the impact of their marketing campaigns by focusing resources on segments who are most likely to convert. This strategic alignment guarantees that marketing budgets are used effectively, resulting in improved conversion rates and sustainable business growth.

As digital technologies improve at a rapid pace, targeted digital marketing options expand. Advanced algorithms and machine learning algorithms enable marketers to forecast customer behavior with greater precision, allowing for real-time campaign modifications and optimizations. Furthermore, the use of artificial intelligence

(AI) improves automation capabilities by automating operations like audience segmentation, targeted content distribution, and performance analytics.

In essence, targeted digital marketing signifies a departure from traditional marketing's broad strokes approach in favor of a more nuanced, data-driven methodology that prioritizes precision and personalization.

Businesses can gain a competitive advantage and engage more deeply with their audiences by harnessing insights from robust data analytics. This promotes long-term engagement, loyalty, and profitability in today's competitive environment.

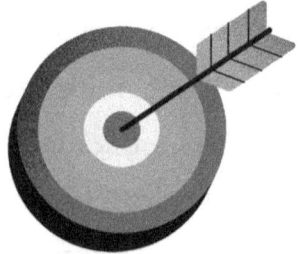

Precision Targeting

Targeted digital marketing matters for several compelling reasons that distinguish it from traditional marketing approaches. Here's a breakdown of why it's crucial and its associated benefits:

Targeted digital marketing excels in its ability to precisely identify and understand specific audience segments. This is achieved through:

- **Demographics:** Understanding basic demographic factors such as age, gender, location, income level, education, and occupation allows marketers to categorize audiences into distinct groups. For example, a luxury fashion brand might target affluent females aged 25-40 in urban areas.

- **Psychographics:** This involves understanding the psychological aspects of consumers, including their motives, values, interests, lifestyle choices, attitudes, and personality traits. Psychographic data provides insights into what drives consumer behavior and purchasing decisions. For instance, knowing that a segment values sustainability and ethical sourcing can guide marketing messages accordingly.

- **Behavioral Data:** Analyzing how consumers interact with your brand online provides valuable insights into their preferences and purchasing habits. This includes tracking browsing patterns, purchase history, content engagement, responses to marketing campaigns, and interactions on social media platforms. For example, if a customer frequently engages with educational content on your website, they might be interested in receiving more informative content or product tutorials.

Targeted digital marketing optimizes return on investment (ROI) by:

- **Efficiency:** By focusing resources on the most relevant audience segments, marketers can reduce wastage on audiences unlikely to convert. This targeted approach ensures that marketing efforts are directed where they are most likely to generate revenue.

- **Cost-effectiveness:** Compared to traditional mass marketing, which can be expensive and less targeted, digital marketing channels such as PPC (Pay-Per-Click) advertising allow for precise budget allocation based on performance metrics. For instance, adjusting bids on keywords that convert well can maximize ROI from search engine marketing campaigns.

- **Measurable Results:** Digital marketing provides robust analytics tools that offer real-time insights into campaign performance. Metrics such as conversion rates, click-through rates, bounce rates, and customer lifetime value (CLV) provide quantitative data to assess the effectiveness of marketing efforts. For example, tracking conversion rates from email campaigns can indicate the success of personalized offers tailored to specific segments.

Enhanced Customer Engagement

Personalized and relevant marketing content enhances engagement by:

- **Tailored Messaging:** By understanding audience preferences and behaviors, marketers can create personalized messages that resonate with consumers. This could include personalized recommendations based on past purchases or content that aligns with consumer interests.

- **Relationship Building:** Engaging with consumers on a personalized level fosters stronger relationships and brand loyalty. For example, responding to customer inquiries on social media or sending personalized thank-you emails after a purchase demonstrates care and enhances the customer experience.

- **Interactive Content:** Utilizing interactive content such as quizzes, polls, and surveys encourages consumer participation and deeper engagement. Interactive elements can also provide valuable data insights into consumer preferences and interests.

Measurable Results

Digital marketing provides powerful analytics tools for:

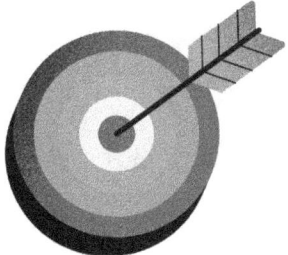

- **Real-time Monitoring:** Unlike traditional marketing methods that may take weeks or months to assess effectiveness, digital marketing allows for real-time monitoring of campaign performance. This enables marketers to make data-driven decisions and adjust strategies promptly.

- **Key Metrics:** Metrics such as website traffic, conversion rates, engagement rates, ROI, and customer acquisition costs provide quantitative data to evaluate campaign success. For example, tracking conversion rates from different ad variations can help optimize campaigns for higher conversion rates.

- **Continuous Optimization:** Analyzing performance metrics allows marketers to identify trends, patterns, and areas for improvement. A/B testing different ad creatives or email subject lines, for example, helps determine which variations resonate best with target audiences.

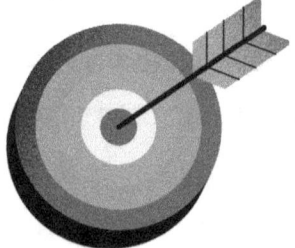

Understanding Your Target Audience

Comprehending Your Target Audience: Profound Observations for Successful Marketing Tactics

Gaining a comprehensive understanding of your target demographic is essential for creating impactful marketing strategies that deeply connect with your prospective customers. This section provides an in-depth analysis of the significance of demographics, psychographics, and behavioral data in obtaining profound understanding of your target audience. It enables organizations to customize their marketing strategies and improve consumer engagement.

1. Demographics Definition and Significance:

Demographic data pertains to measurable attributes of a population or particular subset of individuals. Demographics in marketing offer essential insights into your target audience, enabling you to classify them into several segments based on common characteristics. Important demographic factors encompass:

Age demographics play a crucial role in shaping preferences, purchasing habits, and communication preferences. Various demographic cohorts may exhibit distinct reactions to marketing communications and product offerings.

Gender: Having a comprehensive understanding of gender demographics can have a significant impact on product design, marketing messaging, and promotional techniques that are customized for distinct genders.

Geographic location offers valuable information about regional preferences, cultural influences, and logistical factors for product distribution and marketing efforts.

Income Level: The level of income a person has impacts their ability to buy things and influences their purchasing habits. Wealthier individuals are more likely to allocate a larger portion of their income towards purchasing high-end goods or services, whereas individuals with lesser incomes tend to prioritize affordability.

Education: The educational history of an individual has an impact on their consumer attitudes, interests, and preferences. Individuals with a high level of education may have a preference for receiving in-depth knowledge and appreciate opportunities for intellectual involvement in marketing communications.

Occupation: Occupational demographics provide insights into individuals' professional interests, lifestyle preferences, and purchasing requirements that are associated with particular industries or employment positions.

Application of Marketing Strategies:

Segmentation: Dividing your audience into different demographic groups enables the implementation of focused marketing efforts that are customized to meet the distinct requirements and preferences of each segment.

Personalization: Tailoring marketing communications according to demographic data improves the relevance and impact on various audience segments.

Localization: Localization involves tailoring marketing methods to regional populations to guarantee cultural sensitivity and relevance in global or multi-national campaigns.

Example Application: For example, a company that sells high-end products may focus on attracting wealthy individuals between the ages of 35 and 55, who have a high income and reside in urban regions. Analyze these demographic factors to develop message that highlights exclusivity, high quality, and lifestyle desirability.

2. Psychographics Definition and Significance:

Psychographics explore the underlying psychological elements of consumer behavior, specifically targeting attitudes, values, motivations, interests, lifestyle preferences, and personality characteristics. This qualitative data offers detailed and subtle insights into the factors that influence consumer decisions and preferences.

Understanding the underlying motives and values of your audience is crucial for connecting marketing messaging with their own views and objectives.

Interests and Hobbies: Understanding the interests and hobbies of your audience enables the creation of content and campaigns that really connect with their personal passions and recreational pursuits.

Lifestyle choices refer to the psychographics of an individual, which include their habits, preferences, spending patterns, and social behaviors. These factors greatly influence the way consumers live their lives and make purchasing decisions.

Consumer attitudes and beliefs have a significant role in shaping how brands are perceived and influencing the likelihood of purchasing them. These attitudes extend to not just the brands and products themselves, but also to social concerns and cultural trends.

Personality qualities: Understanding personality qualities such as introversion versus extroversion and risk-taking behavior might enhance our comprehension of customer preferences and decision-making styles.

Application of Marketing Strategies:

Targeting Affinities: By identifying common interests and beliefs, marketers can focus on certain groups of people with personalized messages that evoke strong emotional responses.

material personalization involves tailoring material to match the interests and values of the audience, which improves engagement and cultivates a stronger bond with the business.

Brand Positioning: Brand positioning involves the strategic alignment of brand messaging and values with the beliefs of consumers, which in turn fosters brand loyalty and advocacy among individuals who share similar beliefs.

Example Application: A health and wellness firm that focuses on environmentally aware clients may highlight sustainability, ethical sourcing, and holistic lifestyles in its marketing campaigns. Gaining insight into the psychographics of its audience enables the creation of messages that resonate with their core beliefs and preferences in lifestyle.

Behavioral data refers to the actions and interactions that consumers carry out online. It includes information about their browsing habits, purchase history, engagement with content, answers to marketing campaigns, and interactions on social media platforms. This data is valuable as it provides insights into consumer behavior and preferences. This data-centric strategy provides important insights into consumer preferences and intentions.

Analyzing browsing behavior involves monitoring website visits, tracking pages viewed, and recording travel pathways. This process aids in comprehending consumer interests and product preferences.

Examining previous transactions offers valuable information about purchasing trends, product preferences, and the long-term value of customers (CLV).

Content engagement refers to the process of monitoring the consumption of content, such as reading blog posts, watching videos, or opening emails. This monitoring helps to identify the themes that users find interesting and their level of engagement with the content.

3. Campaign Responses: Assessing the outcomes of marketing campaigns, such as click-through rates and conversion rates, allows for the measurement of effectiveness and provides insights for campaign optimization.

Social media interactions can be monitored to gather feedback on how a brand is seen, how well its content resonates with the audience, and the level of involvement within the community.

Application of Marketing Strategies:

Targeted re-marketing involves retargeting consumers by analyzing their browsing behavior or abandoned carts, which effectively motivates them to make return visits and ultimately leads to conversions.

Personalized recommendations leverage past behavior to boost relevance and maximize cross-selling opportunities.

Segmentation and customization include dividing audiences into distinct groups based on their behavioral data, enabling the implementation of individualized marketing strategies that are specifically designed to cater to individual customer preferences and behaviors.

Example Application: An e-commerce merchant can use behavioral data analysis to identify a specific group of customers who regularly explore fitness equipment but have not yet made a purchase. By utilizing targeted email campaigns that showcase relevant products or special discounts, it is possible to re-engage these clients who have shown a clear interest.

Integration and Application Across Marketing Channels refers to the process of combining and utilizing several marketing channels in a cohesive and coordinated manner.

To achieve a thorough understanding of your target audience, it is important to combine demographic, psychographic, and behavioral data across different marketing channels. This will enable the creation of cohesive and impactful campaigns.

Multi-channel integration refers to the practice of ensuring that messaging and experiences provided to customers are consistent and personalized across many channels, such as websites, social media platforms, and email. This approach helps to reinforce brand identity and enhance customer relationships.

Utilizing data-driven campaigns allows for the optimization of ad targeting, content production, and consumer communication, resulting in increased campaign efficacy and return on investment (ROI).

Continuous optimization involves regularly updating audience profiles using fresh data and market trends to guarantee that they remain relevant and responsive to changing consumer behaviors.

In conclusion,

An in-depth understanding of your target audience, obtained via the analysis of demographics, psychographics, and behavioral data, is crucial for developing precise digital marketing strategies that effectively connect with consumers, foster engagement, and boost conversions.

By utilizing these valuable observations, companies may customize their marketing strategies to cater to the distinct requirements and inclinations of various audience segments, thereby cultivating enduring client connections and ensuring sustained business expansion. Iterative improvement and adjustment guided by data-driven observations guarantee that marketing tactics stay pertinent and efficient in a changing marketplace.

Adopting a comprehensive strategy to comprehending your target audience allows firms to attain marketing success by providing customized experiences and significant interactions that match consumer expectations and desires.

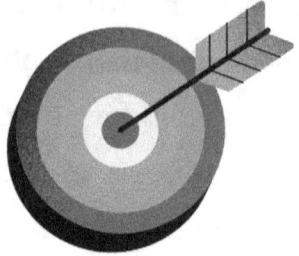

Tools & Resources

In the ever-changing digital marketing landscape, businesses rely on a wide range of tools and resources to efficiently reach and engage their target consumers. Proximity examines key tools and resources required for focused digital marketing campaigns, emphasizing their functions, benefits, and best practices.

1. Google Analytics

Google Analytics is an essential tool for evaluating website traffic and user behavior, giving critical data that guide digital marketing initiatives. Here's a full breakdown of its capabilities and how organizations can use them:

Key features:

Traffic analysis measures the volume and source of website traffic, which includes organic search, sponsored search, direct visits, and referrals.

User Behavior: Examines how users engage with the website, including page visits, session duration, bounce rates, and navigation pathways.

Conversion monitoring: monitoring assesses the efficacy of marketing campaigns by tracking conversions, such as form submissions, purchases, or other targeted behaviors.

Audience Insights: Provides demographic information (age, gender, geography), interests, and technology choices for website visitors.

Benefits:

Data-Driven Decisions: Allows marketers to make informed decisions using real-time data and trends.

Performance Optimization: optimization identifies possibilities to improve website performance, user experience, and conversion rates.

Campaign Evaluation: Determines the ROI of marketing initiatives and modifies strategy to maximize outcomes.

Best practices:

Goal Setting: In Google Analytics, define explicit goals and objectives to accurately assess success metrics.

Customization: Tailor reports, segments, and dashboards to highlight key performance indicators (KPIs) relevant to company objectives.

Continuous Learning: Stay up to date on Google Analytics certifications and training so you can take advantage of advanced features and capabilities.

2. Social Media Analytics:

Social media sites such as Facebook, Instagram, LinkedIn, and Twitter give powerful analytics tools that provide audience demographics, engagement metrics, and campaign efficacy.

Here's a detailed look at how firms can use social media analytics:

Key features:

Audience Demographics: Displays demographic information such as age, gender, geography, and interests of followers and users who engage with content.

Engagement metrics: Uses likes, comments, shares, retweets, and other interactions to assess content success and audience engagement.

Sponsored Campaign Insights: Monitors metrics related to sponsored advertising campaigns, such as reach, impressions, click-through rates (CTR), and cost per acquisition (CPA).

Content Performance: Determines the effectiveness of various content kinds (e.g., videos, photos, links) and publishing schedules in increasing engagement.

Benefits:

Audience Understanding: Enhances understanding of audience preferences, behaviors, and trends in order to adjust content and messaging.

Campaign Optimization: Uses performance data to optimize social media campaigns in order to increase ROI and meet campaign objectives.

Competitive Analysis: analysis compares performance to competitors and industry norms to discover chances for growth.

Best Practices:

Platform-Specific Strategies: Create strategies for each social media platform based on its distinct audience demographics and interaction patterns.

A/B Testing: A/B testing involves experimenting with various content formats, graphics, and messaging to uncover high-performing tactics.

Real-Time Monitoring: Track trends and conversations in real time to seize chances for timely interaction and content development.

3. CRM systems

Customer Relationship Management (CRM) systems concentrate customer data and interactions, allowing firms to create more targeted marketing campaigns and improve customer relationships. Here's a thorough overview of CRM systems in targeted digital marketing.

Key features:

Data Centralization: Combines client information from several touchpoints, such as website interactions, email exchanges, social media engagements, and purchase history.

Segmentation Capabilities: Delivers tailored marketing efforts by segmenting clients based on behavior, preferences, demographics, and lifecycle stage.

Marketing Automation: Automates email marketing, lead nurturing, and customer follow-ups using established workflows and triggers.

Performance Reporting: Creates reports and statistics about marketing effectiveness, lead conversion rates, client retention, and ROI.

Benefits:

Personalization: Provides personalized consumer experiences by delivering relevant content, offers, and communications based on segmented data.

Lead Management: Optimizes lead generation, qualification, and nurturing procedures to boost conversion rates and sales productivity.

Customer Retention: Improves customer loyalty and retention through focused marketing campaigns and individualized engagement techniques.

Best practices:

Integrate CRM systems with other marketing tools and platforms (such as email marketing software and analytics tools) to improve data flow and usefulness.

Data Privacy: Comply with data protection rules (e.g., GDPR, CCPA) by adopting data security measures and gaining consumer consent for data use.

Continuous Improvement: To maximize outcomes, update and adjust CRM strategies on a regular basis based on performance indicators, customer feedback, and market developments.

Effective use of these tools and resources enables organizations to carry out focused digital marketing plans with precision, efficiency, and demonstrable outcomes. Businesses may optimize marketing efforts, maximize ROI, and establish long-term customer relationships by using Google Analytics for website insights, social media analytics for audience engagement, and CRM systems for personalized marketing.

A Continuous monitoring, analysis, and modification based on data-driven insights are critical for remaining competitive in the dynamic digital economy. Embracing these tools improves marketing efficacy while also positioning firms for long-term growth and success in the digital age.

Future Trends

Future applications:

AI and machine learning are set to transform digital marketing by:

Predictive analytics: Advanced computers can analyze massive volumes of data to forecast consumer behavior, allowing marketers to anticipate demands and personalize interactions in real time.

Chatbots and Automation: AI-powered chatbots can answer client questions, make personalized recommendations, and even perform transactions, increasing customer service efficiency.

Information Personalization: Machine learning algorithms may assess user preferences and behaviors to provide highly tailored information, increasing engagement and conversions.

Business Impact:

Efficiency Gains: AI automates monotonous operations, allowing marketers to concentrate on strategy and creativity.

Enhanced Customer Experience: Personalized interactions based on AI insights strengthen customer connections and loyalty.

Competitive advantage: Businesses that use AI can send more relevant and timely marketing messages, exceeding competitors in terms of targeting accuracy and customer happiness.

Voice Search Optimization and Future Trends: Voice search grows with the development of smart speakers and virtual assistants, changing digital marketing techniques.

Natural Language Processing: Marketers must optimize content for long-tail keywords and conversational searches in order to correspond with how people communicate.

Local SEO Optimization: Because voice searches frequently involve local intent, businesses must optimize for local queries and provide correct business information.

Voice Commerce: Because voice assistants facilitate transactions, optimizing for voice search can directly increase sales and conversions.

Impact on Marketing:

SEO Strategy Shifts: Marketers must modify their SEO tactics to capture voice search traffic, concentrating on semantic search and user intent.

New Opportunities: Businesses can develop speech-activated products and services, offering novel ways to interact and help clients via voice interfaces.

Early Adopter Advantage: Brands that adopt voice search optimization early can earn exposure and authority in speech-enabled ecosystems, positioning themselves as leaders in voice commerce.

Future applications for augmented and virtual reality (AR/VR):

AR and VR technology provide immersive experiences that change the way consumers interact with brands.

Product Visualization: Augmented reality allows shoppers to see products in their environment before purchase, improving the shopping experience.

Virtual Try-Ons: In industries such as fashion and cosmetics, VR and AR allow for virtual try-ons, lowering return rates and increasing client satisfaction.

Interactive Marketing Campaigns: Brands may build interactive AR/VR experiences for events, product launches, and marketing campaigns to boost engagement and brand recognition.

Business Opportunities:

Enhanced Engagement: AR/VR experiences capture and excite consumers, resulting in memorable brand interactions that increase engagement and share-ability.

Differentiation: Early adoption of AR/VR can help brands stand out in competitive markets by positioning them as innovative and forward-thinking.

Expanded Reach: Virtual events and experiences may reach worldwide audiences, breaking down geographical barriers and enhancing brand reach and effect.

Blockchain Technology and Future Innovations: Blockchain extends beyond cryptocurrency, providing openness and security in digital marketing:

Ad Transparency: Blockchain can authenticate ad delivery and performance, lowering ad fraud and ensuring that marketers receive what they pay for.

Data Privacy: Blockchain-based solutions can give users ownership over their data, increasing confidence and ensuring compliance with privacy legislation.

Smart Contracts: By automating contract execution using blockchain technology, marketers, publishers, and consumers can simplify payments and agreements.

Business Benefits:

Trust and Transparency: Blockchain's decentralized ledger improves brand-consumer trust by maintaining data integrity and transaction transparency.

Fraud Prevention: By eliminating intermediaries and authenticating transactions, blockchain lowers the risk of fraud while increasing the efficiency of digital advertising.

Regulatory Compliance: By providing immutable records of consent and data usage, blockchain can help organizations comply with data privacy rules such as GDPR.

Customer Experience (CX) Optimization Future Strategy:

CX optimization aims to provide seamless and tailored experiences across all customer touchpoints:

Omni-channel Integration: Integrating data and interactions across channels results in consistent messages and personalized experiences.

Predictive Analytics: AI-powered analytics offer proactive customer service and personalized recommendations that anticipate client demands.

Emotional Engagement: Using AI and data analytics to understand client emotions and preferences improves emotional bonds and loyalty.

Business Impact:

Brand Loyalty: Excellent CX encourages consumer loyalty and advocacy, resulting in repeat purchases and recommendations.

Competitive Differentiation: Businesses that focus CX get a competitive advantage by providing exceptional customer service and tailored experiences.

Long-term Relationships: Personalized CX leads to increased customer lifetime value (CLV) and sustainable business growth.

Conclusion of Future Outlook

AI, voice search, AR/VR, blockchain, and CX optimization are all contributing to the rapid evolution of targeted digital marketing. Businesses that adopt these technologies and trends can reap major benefits:

Innovation Leadership: Early adoption of innovative technology positions organizations as industry leaders, establishing standards for customer interaction and experience.

Competitive Advantage: Leveraging AI for predictive analytics, optimizing for voice search, integrating AR/VR experiences, safeguarding transactions with blockchain, and emphasizing CX optimization help firms stand out in crowded markets.

Improved ROI: By providing more relevant and tailored experiences, organizations may boost conversion rates, increase customer satisfaction, and maximize marketing ROI.

Overall, maintaining current with future trends and incorporating breakthrough technologies into focused digital marketing strategies will be crucial for firms seeking to flourish in a dynamic and competitive digital marketplace.

Embracing these developments not only improves campaign performance, but also fosters long-term client relationships, resulting in corporate success.

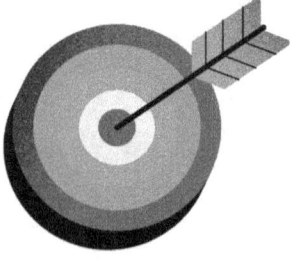

Proximity: Closing Thoughts

As we look ahead to the future of targeted digital marketing, one thing is crystal clear: the landscape is about to undergo significant shift. Businesses are receiving unparalleled insights into consumer behavior and preferences because to advances in artificial intelligence, machine learning, and data analytics. This influx of data enables marketers to hyper-personalize their campaigns, delivering information and offers that are relevant to each individual.

Furthermore, the growth of privacy laws and consumer expectations is influencing the future of targeted marketing. As worries about data privacy grow, marketers must strike a fine balance between personalization and user privacy rights. This paradigm shift is driving the business toward more open and ethical practices, emphasizing trust and value exchange between brands and consumers.

Moving forward, the convergence of digital channels and the proliferation of linked devices will continue to reshape how marketers interact with their customers. From voice search to augmented reality, the channels for reaching consumers will expand, requiring marketers to constantly adapt and innovate. Embracing these technologies not only improves targeting capabilities, but it also offers up previously imagined options for innovation and customer connection.

In summary, the future of targeted digital marketing is a mix of opportunity and responsibility. Businesses may establish deeper connections with their consumers while protecting their privacy by embracing the power of data-driven insights in an ethical and responsible manner. As we navigate these exciting times, remaining nimble, knowledgeable, and consumer-centric will be critical to success in the ever-changing digital marketing ecosystem.

www.ingramcontent.com/pod-product-compliance
Lightning Source LLC
Chambersburg PA
CBHW072055230526
45479CB00010B/1090